PET OWNER'S GUIDE TO THE
DWARF RABBIT

Hazel Leewood

RINGPRESS

Photography: Keith Allison.

Published by Ringpress Books,
Vincent Lane, Dorking, Surrey,
RH4 3YX, England.

First published 1999
© Interpet Publishing. All rights reserved

ISBN 1 86054 121 6

Printed and bound in Hong Kong by Printworks International

CONTENTS

1

INTRODUCING DWARF RABBITS 7

What is a rabbit?; Domestic history; Hobby development; Dwarfs and Mini Lops; Dwarfism; Problem dwarfs.

2

CHOOSING A PET DWARF RABBIT 15

Suitability; Which breed?; Age and sex; Sexing; How many?; Where to purchase; Inspecting the rabbit.

3

SETTING UP HOME   25

Housing space; The bigger the better; Cages; Hutches; DIY Hutch; Furnishings; Location; Exercise pens.

4

CARING FOR YOUR DWARF RABBIT 33

Feeding; Major dangers; Coprophagy; Staple foods; Hay; Fresh foods; Quantity; Cleaning up; Heat stress; Cold weather; Handling; Grooming; Bathing; Training your rabbit (House-training; Precautions; Other pets; Playing).

5

DWARF AND MINI RABBIT BREEDS 49

The Breeds (Polish (British); Netherland Dwarf; Britannia Petite; Dwarf Hotot; Polish (American); Jersey Wooly; Holland Lop; Mini Dwarf Lop; American Fuzzy Lop; Mini Rex; Dwarf Lop; Cashmere Lop; Mini Lop); Colours and patterns.

6

BREEDING 63

Drawbacks; Initial stock; Mating; Gestation; Nestboxes; Diet; The litter; Rearing; Identification; Records; Exhibition; National organisations.

7

HEALTH CARE 75

Strategy (Hygiene; Clinical signs; Reaction); Quarantine; Heatstroke; Stress; Syndromes; Useful data.

1 Introducing Dwarf and Mini Rabbits

Gentle-natured, appealing, cuddly, clean, and low in cost to keep, the dwarf and mini rabbit breeds are very much the direction in which the pet rabbit hobby has been steadily moving during the last few decades. The trend is likely to continue into the foreseeable future. These pint-sized pets start life as everything you could want in a rabbit – and stay that way throughout adulthood. They have brought a new dimension to rabbit-keeping. This is because most of them live within the comfort of their owners' homes. Here, they display their true character, which can only be fully appreciated by having an ongoing and close relationship with a pet. This is much more readily achieved if the pet spends its time in the family home rather than in a hutch at the bottom of the garden or in an outbuilding.

In line with the growth in the number of in-home pets, there has been a growth in the range of housing and other products now available for them. These overcome all the past problems related to keeping rabbits in the home, such as the odours from wooden hutches, which were very difficult to keep odour-free.

Breeders and exhibitors also find the dwarf and mini breeds appealing. Not only is there a better pet market for them, but their small size keeps housing and rearing costs down. A decent-sized stud can be maintained in a smaller area than would be the case with the larger breeds. Dwarfs and minis are easier to transport to shows and make delightful exhibition animals.

WHAT IS A RABBIT?
Although it is such a popular pet, the zoological standing of the rabbit is not well known by the average hobbyist. For many years

it was thought that the rabbit was a rodent, but this is not the case; it differs from rodents in a number of ways, the most obvious being its dentition. Rodents have a single pair of incisor teeth in their upper jaw, while rabbits have a double pair – one set behind the other.

The fact is that rabbits are more closely related to hoofed and other animals than they are to rodents, from an evolutionary standpoint! Their closest relatives are hares and pikas, and, with these, they are placed in the scientific order (a group of related animals) called Lagomorpha. There are 47 species of wild rabbit, but only one of these is the ancestor of the domestic form. This is the Old World or European rabbit, which has the scientific name of *Oryctolagos cuniculus*. 'Orycto' is Greek and means a 'dug out' or 'digger', while 'lagus' (also Greek) means 'a hare'. The word 'cuniculus' is Latin, and means 'rabbit' or 'underground passage'. Zoologically, there are a number of differences between rabbits and hares, but the terms are used rather indiscriminately in popular parlance. For example, the Jack Rabbit of the USA is a hare, while the Belgian Hare is a rabbit.

DOMESTIC HISTORY

The wild European rabbit is thought to have originally been distributed only in the Iberian Peninsula of South West Europe, but has been established in many countries and islands throughout the world by human introduction and gradual expansion. It was first noted by the Phoenicians of about 800 BC, who were quick to appreciate its food value. They traded it in North Africa and throughout the lands bordering the Mediterranean Sea, including Italy.

The Romans bred rabbits in large numbers and kept them in walled gardens called 'lepororii', and thus commenced the process of domestication. As the Roman legions marched across Europe, the rabbit went with them. However, it was the 11th-century Normans of France that took rabbits in large numbers to Britain. They established warrens for them to be kept in for hunting purposes.

Given the famed reproductive capacity of rabbits, it is perhaps surprising that rabbits remained a costly meat item for a few centuries. However, by the 16th century, many monasteries, especially in France, were

The dwarf and mini rabbit breeds are ideal family pets, and are small enough to keep in the house.

beginning to establish mutational colours and forms. Domestication can be regarded as having been completed by about this time, which also marks the time when breeds, of basic types, started to evolve.

HOBBY DEVELOPMENT

Although rabbits have been maintained under domestic conditions for about 2,000 years, it has only been in the last 200 or so that keeping them purely as pets started to become fashionable. Prior to that, they were merely food and fur animals, much like sheep, cattle and other farm livestock, though no doubt some were kept as children's pets.

During the 19th century, there was a great upsurge of interest in keeping many animals for their companion (rather than utilitarian) value, so pet hobbies really began to develop at about this time. Owners were beginning to take a much keener interest in retaining long-established varieties, and also in developing new ones. With these objectives in mind, clubs were formed to cater for the needs of the growing numbers of owners, and shows were organised so breeders could compare their stock.

Breeds, by today's standards, did not exist. There were long-haired, spotted, black, white, lop-eared and other varieties, many of which were named for the area or country from which they came – Flemish, Belgian, Dutch and so on. What the clubs did was to lay down written standards of conformation for this assemblage of forms and colours. Together with the keeping of records, the result was the emergence of true breeds, rather than general types. Most of the rabbit breeds seen today trace back only to the early years of the 20th century, and many are very much younger than that, especially the dwarfs and mini breeds.

DWARFS AND MINI LOPS

In the early years of the hobby, the trend was generally for medium to large breeds. This is not surprising given the fact that the hobby developed directly from breeders

Above: The roots of most dwarf breeds lie with the Polish.

whose primary objective was to produce large meat and fur breeds. However, with the passing of time, more and more breeders whose interest lay only in producing exhibition and pet stock became established. Colours and their patterns, together with ear and fur types, became progressively more important for the growing pet owner and exhibition markets.

As might be expected, smaller breeds, such as the Dutch or English, proved to be a better pet proposition than the large heavy breeds, such as the Beveren, Flemish Giant, Chinchilla and others in the 4.5 kg (10 lb) and above category. While the medium to small breeds were the mainstay of the pet hobby in the years that followed World War II, there were two truly tiny breeds in the wings. These were developed primarily in Germany, Holland and Britain. They were called the Polish and the Netherland Dwarf (why the Polish was so named has never been satisfactorily established). Both were larger than their namesakes of today, and both were viewed with scepticism by long-established rabbit breeders. It is from the Polish that the Netherland Dwarf was probably

The Netherland Dwarf was developed from the Polish, and has been used in numerous crossings to create new dwarf breeds

developed. Most of the present-day dwarf breeds originate from crossings of the Netherland to other breeds, including the lop-eared breeds. These are all discussed in a later chapter.

DWARFISM

The term 'dwarf' in rabbits is descriptive without being precisely defined. Genetically, there are two types of dwarfs in rabbits. In one of these, the gene creating it is fatal, meaning those that inherit it die at birth or shortly afterwards. This form of mutation is not seen in the rabbit hobby. The other type is polygenic, and it is this form that has given us the various dwarf and mini breeds (the term 'mini' is an alternative to 'dwarf' that is applied to some breeds).

Dwarf breeds did not suddenly appear, as with major gene

mutations, but were developed over a period of time by always mating the smallest individuals, thus bringing together more and more of the polygenes for smallness. The effect of polygenic dwarfism is that it alters the shape of the head, which is foreshortened in the smallest of breeds. The ears are also short. The legs, however, remain straight and proportionate to body size and are not unduly short or bowed, as is the case with dwarfs in many other animals derived from a major single gene for dwarfism.

In actual fact, the dwarf breeds are small only in comparison with most other domestic rabbits, and not with their wild ancestors. These have a weight range of 1-2.5 kg (2.2-5.5 lb), corresponding to the weight of the dwarfs. By

The mini lops, also originating from the Netherland Dwarf, are becoming increasingly popular.

comparison, 53 of the approximately 65 rabbit breeds recognised in Britain or the USA have weights that exceed (often considerably) that for wild rabbits. The smallest wild rabbit makes even the dwarf breeds look large. The Porto Santo rabbit (of the island near Madeira) is a subspecies of the European rabbit and rarely exceeds 500 g (1.1 lbs).

For the purposes of this book, a dwarf or mini breed is any breed that carries this term in its name, or any breed that was developed by hybridisation to a dwarf breed.

Using this definition, weight is not a criterion. Some small breeds, such as the Dutch, Himalayan and Thrianta, are lighter and as small as some of the mini breeds. At this time, there are more dwarf breeds with official Standards in the USA than in Britain. This does not mean that these breeds are not available in the UK, and no doubt in due course they will become standardised.

All present dwarf breeds are therefore included, and the future will see many more being developed.

The characteristics of the dwarf breeds include short ears and a foreshortened face. The legs are straight and in proportion to the body.

PROBLEM DWARFS

The breeding strategy used in developing the original dwarfs gave priority to small size. Temperament, conformation and breeding vigour were not initially given the attention they should have received. As a consequence, the Netherland Dwarf, in particular, gained a reputation for being both an unreliable breeder and one with a temperament that left a lot to be desired. Notwithstanding such problems, the breed held great appeal for many hobbyists who saw it had

tremendous potential if its weaknesses could be overcome.

This has been achieved by judicious breeder selection of only the very best examples to breed from. The result is that the pint-sized breeds of today are generally reliable breeders, with temperaments to match. This does not mean that there are no bad examples. Diminutive pets in any species are always potentially more nervous and difficult to breed than are those that are larger. Buyers must exercise due care when purchasing dwarf or mini breeds.

Choosing A Pet Dwarf Rabbit

Rabbits, especially the small ones, make wonderful pets. However, this does not mean they are suited to all households. Potential owners should carefully consider what ownership means before they purchase one. In many instances, rabbits are bought on an impulse in a pet shop, often because a small child wants one. This is never a good way to start. The proof of such folly is evident in the growing number of rabbits found in animal shelters – taken there by uncaring owners who, through selfishness and ignorance, purchased a rabbit without giving full thought to what this entailed.

So, the first thing you must consider is if a rabbit is indeed suited to your situation. If it is, its purchase should not be rushed. When anything is bought in haste, it carries a considerable risk of proving to be a mistake. This is certainly true where pets of any kind are concerned.

SUITABILITY

Many parents assume a little rabbit will make a fine pet for their young children, but this is true only for children above a certain age. No animal is a toddler's pet, and certainly not one as benign as a rabbit. As a general guide, children should be at least seven or eight before they are old enough to handle a rabbit without risking either injury to it, or being injured themselves by raking rear feet claws if they fail to handle it correctly.

A child should not be expected to be wholly responsible for feeding and cleaning their pet. The parent must always take the ultimate responsibility in ensuring all of the pet's needs are met on a daily basis. Rabbits are very social animals, and to be fully appreciated it is important that they interact with humans as much as possible. If you spend a lot of time away from home, the rabbit is not a suitable pet.

While the dwarf and mini breeds are much the best choice for in-home living, they can also be kept outdoors. However, it is absolutely vital, if this is the case, that their housing is of the highest standard with regard to insulation. They should really be protected under a large overhead canopy or within a suitable outbuilding. Being so small, the tiny breeds can readily succumb to excess heat or cold.

WHICH BREED?

If you have decided you would make a good rabbit owner, the next thing is to decide on the

Temperament and health are of paramount importance when choosing a pet rabbit.

breed. Factors to take into account are:

- Longhaired breeds require daily grooming because their hair will otherwise rapidly become matted and full of tangled debris. Young children may place sticky sweets in it. Consider these breeds only if you are really sure you have the time, the patience and the environment suited to them.
- The lop-eared breeds are more at risk of ear problems (parasites, cuts and other wounds) than are the erect-eared breeds. Young children may pull their ears, as might other pets. Once again, the environment should be a factor to consider – especially with longhaired lop-eared breeds.
- Although you may be told that this or that breed has a less reliable temperament than another breed, you should not let this influence your potential choice of breeds. The fact is, you can find bad-tempered individuals in every breed. Much depends on the quality of their breeding and on the way they are reared. You will more likely find questionable natures in the most popular breeds, because of the greater number

of mediocre breeders concerned more about numbers of offspring than their quality. You must be prepared to select carefully, and view a number of litters, if needs be. Colour pattern, while important, should never be rated over temperament or health. Some colours will not be readily available, just as some breeds may not be. You must decide if you are prepared to take alternatives, or wait until the breed and the preferred pattern can be located.

AGE AND SEX

Do not consider obtaining a small breed until the animal is at least seven weeks old. If it is sold when younger, it is at a much greater risk of illness due to the stress of moving home and the fact that its immune system will not be fully effective. The extra seven to ten days can make a great deal of difference to a baby dwarf rabbit.

The male (buck) is generally considered a better pet than the female (doe). He is often more gentle. However, he may also start to spray when he is adult, though this can be overcome by neutering. Likewise, a female can be spayed, but it is a more expensive operation, being more complicated. However, it removes

The rabbit you buy should be at least seven weeks of age.

the risk of phantom pregnancies and aggression resulting from these.

If the pet is to be kept in the home, then neutering/spaying is strongly recommended, as it will overcome such problems – discuss it with your vet.

SEXING
It can be difficult to sex young rabbits, but the procedure is as follows. Place the youngster on its back in the palm of your hand, being sure it is comfortably supported. Now its genital region can be inspected with the free

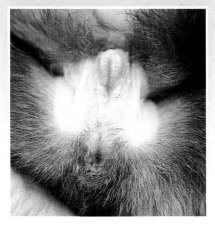

Female.

Male.

hand. Using two fingers, apply gentle pressure to the genital opening. If this appears as a circle with a round tip, it is a male. The female genital opening appears like a slit. Sexing adults will be easy because the male's testicles will be evident.

HOW MANY?

Contrary to what might be thought, given the fact that they are very social creatures in the wild, rabbits are best kept as single pets under domestic conditions. In the wild, they have unlimited space in which to move, and can choose their own companions. When fighting breaks out, they can retreat to a safe distance if they are timid individuals. These conditions are not normally found within pet

environments. As a result, adults housed together in a cage may fight very savagely. This applies to either two bucks or two does.

A male and a female would, of course, be continually mating. The litter could not be left with an adult buck present, because the doe would probably kill the offspring. If the pets are neutered, things change somewhat, because their sexual drives are reduced. But even then, it is best if they have been reared together from their youngest days. If you wish to provide a companion for your rabbit, the best advice would be to obtain a guinea pig. This will cohabit without problems with a rabbit, and, with the dwarf rabbits, there will not be a great difference in size.

19

If you buy two rabbits, you must have the space to accommodate them.

Two adult rabbits can live in harmony if they have lots of space in which to run around, and large living quarters. But first-time owners are strongly recommended to purchase just one pet.

WHERE TO PURCHASE

From a convenience viewpoint, a good pet store is where most people will go to when wanting a small rabbit. The emphasis must be on 'good', meaning a clean store in which the pets are housed under excellent conditions and where the staff have an in-depth knowledge of the pets they sell.

They should guarantee the rabbits sold as dwarfs are exactly that, and come from dwarf parents. They should know the age of the youngsters.

Rarely will you find a high-quality dwarf in a pet store. Such stores are all about average-priced individuals that will make nice pets, without being up to exhibition or breeding standards. The range of colours and patterns will be limited to what they have at any one time. Visit a number of stores if you have particular preferences.

The other obvious source is a breeder. If you want quality and/or a specific colour pattern, and a supplier who really does know about the breed of your choice, then this is the source you should choose. Bear in mind that there are good and bad breeders.

Check for the all-important signs of good health before making your choice.

Seek out one who maintains a good stud, and, preferably, who specialises in the pattern you want. A breeder will know the exact age of the youngsters.

You could also visit an animal shelter, and maybe obtain a nice rabbit that is in need of a good home. However, you will not find many dwarfs or mini lops in such places, and you can never be too sure of any bad habits they may have acquired, or, indeed, much at all about their background.

INSPECTING THE RABBIT

The whole enjoyment of your dwarf rabbit will be spoilt if you do not ensure it is in the peak of good health. Inspect it carefully. The following are the points to look for.

- It should be active, and display no problems that impede its ability to hop.
- Its eyes should be round and bright, never cloudy, nor partially closed and discharging liquid.

Look for bright eyes, a dry nose, and a well-muscled body.

- The nose should be dry and not discharging liquid or mucus. It should not be swollen.
- Ears should be free from parasites, as should the fur. Using your hand, brush the fur against its lie and you will soon notice if parasites are present. The fur should look healthy, not dry and listless.
- The front paws should never be wet, matted and stained. This would indicate a potentially major and lethal problem – the rabbit has been continually wiping its nose to remove a mucous discharge.
- The anal region should be clean and not stained or congealed with faecal matter; that, again, indicates a present or recent problem.
- The body should be well muscled, never skinny nor pot-bellied, which would indicate worms.

- It is very important in the dwarf breeds that the teeth are inspected. The upper incisors should just touch and overlap those of the bottom jaw. If the upper teeth protrude, creating a gap between upper and lower, this is a bad fault, called 'overshot'. If the lower teeth protrude, this is even worse, and is called 'undershot'. Both conditions will result in overgrown teeth and difficulty in eating correctly. Never purchase such rabbits.
- The youngster should not display any form of aggression or nervousness, but should be quite happy to be handled. Excitable babies indicate poor temperament or lack of breeder handling. You cannot be sure which is the case, but it does not matter because such individuals are best avoided.

Setting Up Home

Choosing a suitable home for your pet must reflect whether it is to live indoors (which would include an outbuilding) or outdoors. The range of available homes in both instances is extensive.

Always obtain the rabbit's housing before purchasing the pet. This enables you to look around for just the right unit. When this is found, it can be furnished so you are then able to devote your time to seeking the ideal resident for it.

You should invest in spacious, well-constructed accommodation that is easy to clean. Avoid low-cost hutches and cages – they will have limited wear life and, especially where outdoor hutches are concerned, they will be unsuitable.

The housing for your pet will be the most expensive item, and should be a major priority.

HOUSING SPACE

The housing space a rabbit will need should be influenced by the amount of time it is likely to be allowed out of its cage for exercise. An in-home pet given many hours of freedom, or an outdoor pet that has the benefit of a generous exercise run, will not need quite the same sized hutch or cage (though this would be ideal) as the rabbit that spends the greater part of a day in its housing.

THE BIGGER THE BETTER

A rabbit home can never be too large, but it can be, and often is, too small. As a guide, the minimum cage or hutch size should be 62 x 45 x 38 cm (24 x 18 x 15 in). This would be suitable for one dwarf. Its height allows the pet to sit upright, as rabbits often do to see what is going on.

A cage suitable foa a dwarf rabbit that is to be kept in the home.

CAGES

These will be made from galvanised weldmesh of various thickness and quality. The most costly are those with an epoxy resin or chromium covering, both of which are easier to keep clean and far more aesthetically pleasing than bare metal, but are also more expensive.

The floor to the cage may be of three types: weldmesh with a hole size of 1.25 cm (0.5 in) squared, slatted wood or plastic, or a solid material. Wire floors have a sliding tray beneath them so that uneaten food and faecal matter can fall though and be readily removed, thus having apparent (rather than real) hygiene benefits. However, such floors are the least suited to any animal and are not recommended. Apart from causing

sores to the feet, they are uncomfortable.

Slatted floors are better on both accounts, but a solid floor is best. Not only is it more natural, but it allows the rabbit to eat caecal pellets voided from the anus (these are discussed in the feeding chapter). The solid floor may be fitted with a sliding tray that can easily be removed for thorough cleaning. It can be replaced when it becomes worn, thus saving the cage floor from wear.

Some cages are comprised of a weldmesh frame clipped on to a plastic base. Most of these are too small to provide a sleeping area in the form of a nestbox. Nor do they provide any space for the rabbit to move around in, taking account of its litter pan and food bowls. However, if you can locate a very large one, it will serve its purpose for the in-home pet. Some of the better commercially made units come complete with legs and are designed specifically for the house pet.

The door to a cage may be on the front, the top, or both. The key feature of this is that it should be large enough for you to easily reach in and lift the pet out. It should be fitted with a secure childproof lock, if this is appropriate.

Wire cages can be purchased as complete or ready-to-assemble units. The handy person could

also design and make their own cage using the various-sized panels that can be purchased from pet shops, or speciality suppliers who advertise in rabbit magazines.

HUTCHES

The range of hutches is more extensive than that of cages. It is best to view many styles before investing in one. If the hutch is for an indoor location, it need not be quite as robust as one that must withstand wind, rain and all else that a temperate climate may throw at it. This said, some of the thin, flimsy plywood units sold as

There is a wide variety of hutches to choose from.

hutches are best ignored. They certainly were never made for long-term wear by anyone who knew anything about rabbits!

The basic hutch should comprise a sleeping area and separate feeding and toilet compartment. If the feeding area is extensive, it will provide some limited exercise space. The front of the hutch should have a solid door opening to the sleeping compartment, and the rest of the front facade will be of weldmesh of 2.5 x 2.5 cm (1 x 1 in) maximum hole size. This can be mounted on a frame that can be removed, or as a large door to facilitate cleaning.

It is very useful to include a 10 cm (4 in) high removable board across the front of the hutch, behind the weldmesh frame, and behind the sleeping compartment door. This is to prevent shavings and debris falling out of the hutch. It also acts as a safety barrier for the pet when the front is removed for cleaning. In a large hutch, a separate access door can be included to give easy feeding access without having to remove the entire front panel.

DIY HUTCH

As with wire cages, if you are a handy person, you could design and make your own hutch. Do not use chicken wire for either hutches or exercise pens. It has limited life and cannot be kept taut: it always looks rather crude. Whether indoors or out, the hutch should always be placed on legs, so there is plenty of under-floor ventilation. The legs should be 23 cm (9 in) or more in height.

If the hutch is to be sited outdoors, it should be made from wood of about 1.25 cm (0.5 in) in thickness so that it will insulate against heat and cold. Its roof should have an overhang all the way around, and should slope from front to rear to rapidly remove rain. It will also need a good roofing felt. The exterior walls of a hutch should be treated with a preservative, which should be re-coated every year to ensure longest life. The inside can be painted with a non-lead gloss so it is easily wiped.

FURNISHINGS

The house furnishings will be a floor covering and food and water vessels. The floor should be covered with shavings obtained from pet shops. This ensures they will not be contaminated with either chemicals or potential

Hay doubles up as a food item and as soft bedding.

A gravity-fed water bottle should be attached to the cage or hutch bars.

Heavy ceramic bowls cannot be tipped over or chewed.

pathogens (parasites, fungal spores), as might be the case with those obtained direct from lumberyards. Pine should never be used, as it has been proven to be dangerous to small mammals due to its high phenol content. This is harmful to a rabbit's respiratory and other systems.

On top of the shavings, a generous amount of fresh hay should be placed in the sleeping compartment. This is most important, because it is both a food item and soft bedding. It must be replenished daily. Straw has no value as a food item, as bedding or as a floor covering, and its stiff, sharp ends can cause eye and ear injuries. Sawdust is too fine as a floor covering, and can irritate the nostrils, ears and anal area. Plain sheets of brown paper can be placed under the shavings and will absorb any urine not soaked up by them. An excellent floor covering is the natural fibre type made from wood pulp. It carries no health risks and minimises odours. The drawback is cost, which is high compared to shavings.

The drinking vessel for most rabbits will be the inverted bottle type. These are easily clipped to the cage or hutch bars. It is best to purchase the better brands as these will not leak so readily, nor be so easily chewed. Open water pots still have value, but must be of the heavy earthenware type, otherwise your rabbit will soon tip them over.

Food should likewise be given in heavy pot dishes. Those made of plastic will be chewed, as well as thrown around the hutch either in fun or in anger (built-up nervous energy and stress). Hay can be placed into hayracks that can be fitted to hutches, if the hutch is large enough.

LOCATION

It is important that a cage or hutch should be situated in a location that will provide the pet with the most comfortable and healthy living environment. In a home, this means not facing doors that may cause draughts, nor placed where the cage will be subject to fluctuating temperatures. These places will be where sunlight falls on the cage for long periods of time, or close to heating or cooling units. It is best that the cage is well above floor level, as this will not only make daily chores easier but will allow the pet to see what is going on when confined to its cage.

The outdoor hutch should be sited so that it may enjoy early morning sunshine, but be in shadow by or before midday. This then reduces the risk of excess heat, which can be very dangerous to a rabbit in a confined space.

The hutch should be protected from cold winds and rain. This can be done by placing it under a wooden or similar canopy. This will have the added advantage of enabling the owner to attend to chores with minimum discomfort. It is best to site the hutch on a solid surface, such as paving stones, so that debris can be easily cleaned up.

EXERCISE PENS

If you have a totally secure

garden, your pet will greatly enjoy exercising in it, but always under supervision, in case a local cat spots the rabbit. Supervision will also ensure that the pet does not eat all your cherished flowers or other vegetation that it decides taste nice. If you wish to let the pet enjoy the outdoors, but not under continuous supervision, you could easily make a playpen where it can spend many happy hours, even when there are small showers.

The pen can be as large, especially in length, as you wish. Staple weldmesh mesh on to a frame to make one or more panels, which can be hinged or bolted together. The pen should have a weldmesh top and floor (if it is to be placed on lawn or earth), so the rabbit cannot tunnel out. The wire roof is to prevent cats or dogs from jumping in. At one end, feature a covered area with a solid floor and front weatherboard. The pet can retreat to this if it gets too hot or if it rains. The pen can be moved from one location to another so the rabbit can graze fresh grass, and it should always contain a water bottle.

Of course, you could build a permanent run with a solid concrete or slab floor. In this, you could include rocks, logs and tunnels the pet would really enjoy. All pets should have access to exercise pens so they can benefit, physically and mentally, from the outdoors and the feel of fresh air, sunshine and breezes.

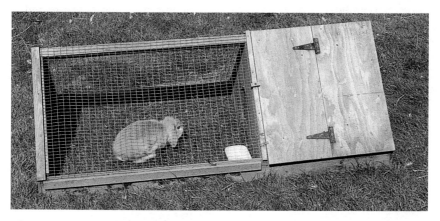

A secure outdoor exercise area will be much appreciated.

4 Caring For Your Dwarf Rabbit

Once the new pet has arrived in your home, it should be placed in its housing and left to rest. Changing homes is a very traumatic experience for a young rabbit suddenly taken away from its siblings or other companions. It should always be spoken to in a soft, reassuring voice. Children should be educated to treat the new pet with respect, not to wake it from sleep or rest periods, and to leave it alone when it is feeding.

FEEDING
Rabbits are extremely cosmopolitan in their diet, meaning that they will eat most plant matter. They will also accept quite a range of foods that are animal by-products, such as milk, cheese, beef extracts and their like.

Considerable research has been done on the nutritional requirements of these animals, and today there is a range of complete diets available that take much of the guesswork out of feeding. However, scientific information and complete diets are not without drawbacks. They can tend to encourage owners to feed a monotonous menu and to focus on certain vitamins, minerals and food compositions to the point that these may be supplied out of all proportion to their actual needs. An excess of calcium, selenium, iron, vitamins etc. can be every bit as dangerous as a shortage of them, and the same applies to proteins, carbohydrates and fats.

What should also never be forgotten is that food not only provides the nutritional essentials for healthy growth, but also mental stimulation, and, therefore, psychological wellbeing. The aroma, sight, relative texture and taste of a food are important to your rabbit. They allow it to exercise choice, and enjoy favoured flavours rather than be confronted with the same items day after day. I have never seen a rabbit get excited about a bowl of pellets, but they will prance about in obvious joy and anticipation when they know you are bringing them a bowl with a range of their favourite items in it.

The key to dietary success lies in utilising all that animal nutritionists can tell us about ingredient needs, then supplying them in a way that will ensure peak health, yet not take away the pet's ability to make choices and to enjoy some food items in their natural state.

MAJOR DANGERS

From the outset, if you are aware of nutritional dangers you will be less likely to allow them to become a reality. Avoid feeding any item that is less than fresh.

Food provides for nutritional needs, but it should also be a source of mental stimulation.

Pellets should be hard, never soft and crumbling. They should smell fresh and be stored in a darkened, dry, well-ventilated cupboard. They must be contained in such a way that they are at no risk of being fouled by rodents. If these conditions are not met, the pellets' nutritional value will be greatly reduced and they may be dangerous due to mould or other pathogenic colonisation.

Hay should likewise be stored in a dry, well-ventilated location that is not subject to direct sunshine, as this will rapidly reduce its vitamin and protein content. Fresh foods (vegetables and fruits) should be rinsed before feeding. They should never be left to sour in the pet's housing, where they will quickly become attacked by bacteria, as well as attracting flies. What is not eaten within about one hour should be removed and discarded.

Never feed any item in a sudden glut, especially fresh foods. This can be dangerous, even lethal, especially to young rabbits, and will result in diarrhoea at the least. Within the digestive system of the rabbit live many bacteria, both beneficial and harmful. If a food item is supplied in a glut, there may be insufficient bacteria to cope with it. The result is a digestive upset and a proliferation of dangerous bacteria. These, especially in the caecum, can create many serious problems that will negatively affect the caecum's ability to function correctly. In turn, this will lead to loss of essential amino acids needed for normal body metabolism.

With these facts in mind, any new food item should be introduced to the diet on a gradual basis, over one or two weeks. At the first sign that diarrhoea is evident, the item should be reduced until the bowels are normal again. It can then be added at a slower rate. It can be very tempting to give your pet too much of something that he clearly enjoys, but, by regulating such items, he will be able to have some, yet not be at risk of illness through gorging on them.

With these comments in mind, it is important that you find out exactly what your new pet is being fed when you collect it. This diet should be maintained until the youngster has settled in, after which time you can make any desired changes, as discussed.

COPROPHAGY
This term applies to the process

whereby rabbits eat what appears to be their own faecal matter. These soft green pellets are actually food items produced in the caecum (a small side chamber of the large intestine) by bacteria. They contain essential amino acids that the rabbit cannot synthesise itself, and which are needed for building protein. Once eaten, they are passed through the digestive system, where their constituents are absorbed into the blood, and then transported to various parts of the body. Rabbits housed on wire mesh floors lose the benefit of these. As a consequence, they require extra protein to compensate for their loss. Medications can have an adverse effect on the caecum, which is why their use without veterinary advice can be very dangerous.

It is most important that the teeth of a rabbit, especially the incisors, are regularly checked. Their teeth grow continuously, and, if they do not wear correctly, they will affect the rabbit's ability to eat what it should. When this happens, the rabbit will lose weight, and the beneficial bacteria of the digestive system, especially in the caecum, will die and compound the situation.

STAPLE FOODS

The staple part of a rabbit's diet should be pellets and hay, which can be given on a free-choice basis. Only if the rabbit becomes obese might you need to ration the pellets, under veterinary advice. Both of these foods contain variable amounts of protein, fat and carbohydrates. Necessary vitamins and minerals are added to pellets, so they provide a complete diet in a convenient form.

Pellets: With pellets, or the more modern kibble-type foods, you should check the label to ascertain what their ingredient percentages are. As a general guide, a rabbit requires 12 to 16 per cent protein and 2 to 4 per cent fat. Some of the commercial pellets produced for meat rabbits contain high protein percentages, 18 to 22 per cent, and should not be used.

A range of pellets is available, and it is always best to obtain the higher-priced brands, if possible. They will have better nutritional content, and so will more readily satisfy the rabbit's appetite than low-cost brands. Some pellets contain hay, but these are not essential if your pet is given ample fresh hay on a daily basis.

STAPLE FOODS

Buy top-quality pellets for
your rabbit.

A mix of cereals, with
pellets mixed in can be fed.

Hay is an
essential part
of a rabbit's
diet.

FRESH FOODS

Shepherd's Purse.

Carrot.

Cabbage.

Groundsel.

An alternative to pellets as the traditional staple food for rabbits (which some breeders still use) is a dry mix of various items. These include oats, wheat, maize, barley, and bran. Oats may be whole or crushed. Many breeders include some pellets in mixes so the rabbit has a nice selection to choose from. However, you must be careful that the pet does not become obese due to the very high carbohydrate content of all cereal crops.

Hay: The importance of hay cannot be overstressed. It is rich in fibre (20 to 25 per cent) and low in calories. It is composed of both digestible and non-digestible parts, and it has the following uses.

- It helps move food along the digestive tract.
- It reduces the risk of blockages, such as hairballs.
- It provides prime energy for the bacteria of the caecum.
- It helps to maintain liquids in the digestive tract.
- It is important in helping to break down foods and also helps to maintain healthy and correct-sized faecal pellets. Undigested hay is voided in faeces.

Hay can be divided into two types – legume and grass.

Leguminous hays include alfalfa, and numerous clovers. These contain 16 to 24 per cent protein and have a high calcium content. By comparison, grass hays contain 8 to 16 per cent protein and much less calcium. On this basis, the grass hays are the best for adult rabbits, while the leguminous ones are better for growing youngsters and breeding females. Actual nutritional content in any hay is greatly influenced by when it is cut (young or older plant) and how it is stored. Straw, which is derived from late cutting of grain plants, has little nutritional value but has excellent fibre content.

FRESH FOODS

Under this heading can be included fruits, vegetables, wild plants and any foods of animal origin. Unlike pellets, all of these foods have a short exposure life. If a rabbit is given a sound diet of pellets (or cubes) and lots of hay, its need for fruit and vegetables is greatly reduced nutritionally, but is very important for other reasons, already discussed. If a rabbit is fed on a dry-mix diet then fresh foods have greater nutritional importance, because they are rich in vitamins.

Useful fresh foods are apple,

A selection of fresh food provides variety in the diet.

potato, beet, turnip, carrot, green cabbage, spinach, dandelion, blackberry and raspberry (including leaves and stem), chicory, chickweed, shepherd's purse, coltsfoot and groundsel, to name but a few. Avoid very liquid foods such as tomatoes, oranges and their like, because they will more readily induce diarrhoea. Lettuce is not so beneficial as its reputation suggests. Never feed plants grown from bulbs and be sure you correctly identify wild plants before feeding them to your pet.

It is always beneficial to supply a rabbit with things to gnaw on.

Branches from fruit trees and trees such as willow are an excellent source; they are all high in fibre. Baked wholemeal bread is another handy item for gnawing.

QUANTITY

Providing your pet is healthy, is given ample free exercise and is under no stress (which is discussed in the health chapter), it will eat only what it needs to remain in healthy condition. On this basis, it can be given pellets and dry mixes on a free-choice basis.

Fresh foods should be carefully rationed. As a guide, supply them as a mixed salad on the basis of about one cup per 2.3 kg (5 lb) body weight per day. Chop the items into small portions. You will soon establish your rabbit's preference order. The best time to feed these foods is in the morning or when you return from work, so you can observe which are the favourites.

To establish the amount of pellets or dry-mix food your pet is eating, weigh a quantity and feed. Twenty-four hours later, weigh what is uneaten, to give a consumed weight. Repeat over a few days, and you will establish normal intake.

This must also be done with the fresh foods. In this instance, you need only obtain the weight of what is consumed within about one hour, after which the food should be discarded before it sours. You now have your rabbit's total intake per day, and the only other figure you will need is the water consumption. If you have a graduated water bottle, it will be easy to read what has been drunk. Water consumption will rise or fall, depending on how much fresh food is consumed, the time of the year (hot or cold) and the activity level of the pet.

CLEANING UP

It is most important that your rabbit's housing is kept in a constant state of cleanliness. If it is not, and especially if it is a wooden hutch, it will soon begin to smell. This apart, it will attract flies, and be very unhealthy for the rabbit. The unwanted odour from rabbit housing derives from the ammonium compounds present in urine and faecal matter.

If the housing is lacking in ventilation, the molecules of ammonia build up and can cause respiratory and other problems by damaging the delicate mucous linings of the nasal passages. Each day, remove any damp floor covering and faecal matter, and give the housing a complete cleaning each week. Be very sure all debris is removed, especially from the corners. Household bleach is an excellent disinfectant and can be used to make a very dilute solution with water. Having used it to clean the hutch and bars or mesh, wipe with warm water to remove any residual chemical. Be sure to allow the housing to dry before renewing the bedding and placing the rabbit back into it.

HEAT STRESS

Rabbits do not cope well with

Your rabbit must be kept in surroundings that are fresh and clean.

undue heat. You must always remember this, especially if the rabbits are kept outdoors. Once the temperature exceeds 75 degrees F (24 degrees C), they will start to become uncomfortable, especially if longhaired or lop-eared. Above 85 degrees F (29 degrees C), they may start to become stressed, with the possibility that they may collapse if the temperature rises beyond this for any length of time.

Outdoor hutches must always be kept cool during very high temperatures. They can be sprayed periodically with water, ice bottles can be placed in the hutch and fans can be directed at one end of the hutch. It may be possible to move the hutch into a more shaded location, or to place a sun canopy over it, if one is not already in use.

Water must be changed twice a day because rabbits do not like warm water. A couple of ice cubes in the bottle will help it to remain cool for longer.

COLD WEATHER

During very cold weather, it is important that the outdoor pet has lots of hay in its sleeping box. The water bottle, or just its spout, may freeze, so be aware of this possibility. The use of a heavy open water pot may be useful at such times. If rain or snow soaks the floor covering, this may freeze. Guard against this possibility by fixing a stiff plastic sheet on to the front of the hutch. Leave some space at the top so fresh air can still circulate.

HANDLING

Never lift a rabbit up by its ears. This is painful and will only panic the rabbit. The way to hold a rabbit is, first, to place a hand over its neck to control it, and then slide your free hand under its stomach and lift, bringing it to your chest. Only when its body weight is not secure will it wriggle and possibly scratch with its rear legs.

Once the rabbit is confident in the way you lift it, you can place its front paws on your shoulder, with one hand supporting its rear end, the other stroking its back. Never let a child clasp both hands around its midriff and attempt to lift it. The rabbit will wriggle and strike out with both front and rear legs, possibly inflicting bad scratches before the child drops the pet. The fall may then injure the rabbit.

GROOMING

Regular grooming not only removes dead hair, but also invigorates the skin and promotes good hair growth. Shorthaired breeds can be brushed and then polished with a soft cloth to give lustre to the coat. Longhaired breeds should be brushed first, then gently combed. Never pull at tags or knots, but tease them apart with your fingers and thumbs, then brush and comb.

If the pet is placed on a table to be groomed, ensure the table has a non-slip mat on it. While grooming, take the opportunity to inspect the fur for parasites, check the ears and teeth. If wax is seen in the ear, it can be removed gently with a cotton bud dampened in lukewarm water. Never probe into the pet's ears, as this could prove dangerous.

The nails will need to be checked as they should not be allowed to grow too long. Nails can be trimmed using guillotine-type nail-trimmers, being careful not to cut too near the quick, or

Regular brushing removes dead hair and promotes new growth.

The longhaired breeds will also need combing.

A programme of training is needed if your rabbit is to be an indoor pet.

the nail will bleed and be very painful to the rabbit. If you are new to rabbit-keeping, ask an expert, or your vet, to show you how to perform this task.

BATHING

Under normal conditions, shorthaired breeds will not need bathing. They keep their coats in superb condition by constant grooming. Should the coat become unduly dirty for any reason, it can be cleaned by sprinkling chalk powder, from the pet store, into the coat. This must then be removed totally by grooming with a medium stiff bristle brush, followed by a fine steel-toothed comb.

The coat of longhaired breeds will attract much more dust and debris, to the degree that periodic bathing may be deemed necessary. In such instances, it is most important that the coat is thoroughly groomed first. If this is not done, then any tags that remain will form mats during bathing. They may prove difficult to remove afterwards and may need to be clipped from the coat.

When bathing, use a mild cat or baby shampoo and ensure that it does not get into the pet's eyes or ears. Stand the rabbit in a large plastic kitchen bowl, or in the sink, which should contain a rubber non-stick mat. Fill with two or three inches of warm water with which to soak the pet's coat.

After shampooing thoroughly, rinse the coat with warm water to remove all trace of shampoo. Next, give the coat a brisk towelling before grooming with the bristle brush. Place the rabbit in a warm location to dry. If placed back in his cage, ensure this contains extra, fresh hay. Do not let the pet outdoors until its coat is thoroughly dry – and then only if the temperature is very warm.

TRAINING YOUR RABBIT

HOUSE-TRAINING

If the rabbit is an indoor pet it can be house-trained, but this needs a great deal of patience and is rarely 100 per cent successful. If its cage is large enough, place a small cat litter tray in it, complete with a biodegradable litter. The pet will probably use this as a toilet, so the beginnings are in hand. Next, restrict the pet's freedom to a single room, and include a litter tray. Whenever it is seen to defecate, gently lift the pet and place it in the tray – which should ideally already contain a few faecal pellets.

It is then a case of repeating this process until the rabbit gets the idea. Never give the pet unrestricted freedom between rooms until it has been trained, and it is advisable to place litter trays at convenient places. Rabbits are not like dogs and cats, which can control their bowel movements readily; litter trays must be convenient for success. You must accept some faecal droppings, but these quickly dry and are easily swept up. Never chastise a rabbit; it simply will not understand why and will become fearful of you.

PRECAUTIONS

Before allowing the pet to wander around your home, take due precautions against dangers. Do not leave harmful chemicals in open tins that the rabbit might tip on to itself. Trailing wires from electrical tools and irons are

Rabbits are lively, inquisitive creatures and they thrive on play and exercise.

another danger if the pet tugs at them, as rabbits are apt to do. Electrical cords should be protected within suitable casings. Indoor plants at low levels may be nibbled and could be poisonous. If not, they may be totally devoured if they have an edible flavour!

Always watch out for through-draughts, which may cause a door to slam on to an unsuspecting rabbit. Likewise, be careful never to leave outside doors open when the pet is roaming.

OTHER PETS

Although rabbits and dogs and cats can become close friends, it is best not to count on it. The appealing photos you see in books show only the pets that do get on, not the thousands of rabbits that are killed or badly injured by dogs and cats each year in homes, or while exercising in gardens. Always supervise interactions between these pets, just to be on the safe side. Rabbits will, however, get on well with guinea pigs.

PLAYING

Unless a rabbit is given ample freedom to exercise, its true character is never really seen. They enjoy dashing around, just as a puppy or kitten will, often clearly in their own little world of fantasy. They will suddenly stop, look around, and, with obvious playfulness in their demeanour, sprint away, often twitching their bodies and kicking their rear legs high into the air, full of the joys of life.

Just as quickly, they will come to a halt and flop down, rear legs stretched out behind them. They will join with you in a game of chase, first being the chaser, then the chased. They will run after small balls, though they soon lose interest in them, and of course will never retrieve them. They can be taught to jump, and, indeed, this has now been developed into a competitive sport in some European countries, though not so much with the dwarf breeds.

Rabbits are very inquisitive animals, always exploring their surroundings. While their intelligence is not comparable to dogs' or cats', they can be taught to respond to their name. They thoroughly enjoy and look forward to interaction with their owners, and it is very sad when one sees these rabbits imprisoned in small hutches and denied the companionship they thrive on.

5 Dwarf And Mini Rabbit Breeds

At this time, there are six dwarf and mini breeds that are Standardised in the UK (meaning they have written Standards) and nine in the USA, giving a total of 13 breeds, allowing for the two that have Standards in both countries. They range in weight from just 1 kg (2.2 lb) to 2.9 kg (6.5 lb). They are seen in a very impressive list of colour patterns, while the fur type may be normal, longhaired, woolly or rex. Ears may be short or medium in length, and are carried erect (seven breeds) or pendent (six breeds).

The descriptions that follow are basic, but sufficient to give an overview of the breed. Potential owners who are thinking in terms of exhibiting should obtain copies of the appropriate Breed Standard from their ruling rabbit association. These describe the breed in detail. They list acceptable colours and patterns, and also major and minor faults.

A few faults in a pet rabbit, which might make it unsuitable for showing, will not be important or detract from it as a pet. Most exhibitions feature classes for pet rabbits. These are judged on health and general appeal rather than against the Standard. Via these, pet owners can still enjoy the thrill of the exhibition side of the hobby. Indeed, many serious exhibitors gained their first feel for showing via the pet classes. From these, the desire to become serious breeders was developed.

THE BREEDS

The following breeds are presented in ascending UK weight. The weight quoted is accurate against the British Standards in pounds, but is rounded up in metric for simplicity. Where a breed is not Standardised in the UK, the American weight is given, again, with the pounds being as per the

Standard. In the USA, the weight range may be slightly different for breeds that have recognition in both countries. The weight given is for ideal and maximum weight individuals. In some Standards, a minimum weight is included, but these are not presented here. Does are often somewhat heavier than bucks in rabbit breeds. The countries (UK and USA) in which they have a written Standard follows the breed name. Most of the breeds are also recognised in many mainland European countries and Canada. Finally, the generally accepted country of origin is given.

Polish: Tends to be excitable.

POLISH (BRITISH)
Standard: UK
Weight: 1-1.2 kg (2-2.5 lb)
Country of Origin: Britain
This is the original dwarf rabbit and was first developed during the mid-19th century. Its origins are debatable, but it was originally a much heavier breed – over 1.8 kg (4 lb). This was considered tiny at the time. It was first exhibited in Hull, England, in 1884, when a class of 17 were on show. In the USA, the breed is called the Britannia Petite to distinguish it from the American Polish.

The Polish is an elegant and lithe breed that has a show stance similar to that of the Belgian Hare – standing upright on its forelegs with an arched back, and lots of space beneath its underbelly. The coat is short and smooth; the ears are short, though somewhat longer and fuller than the Netherland. The head is more oval in profile and should never be round, as in the ideal Netherland.

The breed is available in all colours and patterns, as long as they resemble those of an established breed. It enjoys good support in Britain and Europe. Its main drawback is that it does have a reputation for being excitable – it is essential that, if required as a pet, its temperament is solid. It is not a breed you will often see in a pet store.

NETHERLAND DWARF

Standard: UK and USA
Weight: 1-1.2 kg (2-2.5 lb)
Country of origin: Germany
The second oldest of the dwarfs, this breed was developed from the Polish. In Germany it was called the Hermelin, and was a red- or blue-eyed white, Standardised in 1903. Its first colour varieties

Netherland Dwarf: The most popular of all the dwarf breeds.

were developed in Holland and Standardised in that country during 1940. From Holland it was exported to Britain in 1949, hence its English language name. It arrived in the USA from Britain in about 1965.

In its early years in Britain, the Netherland was dogged with breeding and temperament problems, but these were steadily overcome with the passage of time. The breed is recognised in every colour and pattern seen in rabbits. It is a shorthaired breed, and sports tiny, erect ears that are ideally 5 cm (2 in) in length. The body is short and compact, the legs are straight, and the shoulders are broad. The head should ideally be round, though many of pet quality will display an oval shape. The eyes are large and round.

From its humble beginnings, the Netherland has deservedly become the most popular pet and exhibition rabbit in the world. It has had a greater impact on the hobby than any other breed since the Belgian Hare and the Dutch. This is because it has played such an important role in the creation of other breeds, as well as paving the way for more owners to view rabbits as in-home pets rather than as back garden residents.

BRITANNIA PETITE
Standard: USA
Weight: 1.2 kg (2.5 lb) maximum
Country of origin: Britain
This is the name given in America to the Polish of British type (see above). In the USA, only ruby-eyed white and black otter (which is similar to the tan pattern) are acceptable. As a consequence, this limits the popularity of what is an extremely fine rabbit.

DWARF HOTOT
Standard: USA
Weight: 1.2-1.4 kg (2.5-3 lb)
Country of origin: Germany
The Dwarf Hotot was simultaneously developed in East and West Germany during the mid-1970s from crossings involving Blanc de Hotots (the French parent breed for its pattern) and Netherland Dwarfs. Surprisingly, this attractive breed has never really enjoyed the support its appearance deserves. It has the look of a Netherland but is easily distinguished from this by its eye-band. This is a narrow black band of hair that encircles the eye, which is dark brown. The band should be a complete circle and as even in thickness as possible. The rest of the body is pure white. The ears are short, but slightly longer than in the Netherland. The coat is short and sleek.

POLISH (AMERICAN)
Standard: USA
Weight: 1.1-1.6 kg (2.5-3.5 lb)
Country of origin: USA
Larger than its European namesake, this is very similar in appearance to the Netherland, which was used in its development. Originally, any tiny rabbit of albino type that was produced from the Dutch, Silver and other breeds was often called 'Polish' in the USA. The Polish breed arrived from Britain and was no doubt bred to these other rabbits. The Netherland Dwarf then arrived, and was also bred to the Polish to improve its type and reduce its size. The result was a breed that looked like a Netherland, was called a Polish, but bore little resemblance to the European Polish. As already discussed, the situation was resolved by calling the Polish of British type 'Britannia Petite'.

The breed differs from the Netherland not only in being larger but in having a slightly less round head, somewhat longer ears, and other small differences in its Standard. It is available in a

Jersey Wooly: The smallest of the longcoated breeds.

limited range of colours. It is not a popular breed, but has a small nucleus of supporters.

JERSEY WOOLY

Standard: USA
Weight: 1.4-1.6 kg (3-3.5 lb)
Country of origin: USA
For those who like a breed with a long coat, the Jersey is the smallest. Developed in the state of New Jersey during the 1970s, it is still a young breed, but one that is gaining devotees at a very rapid rate. Its soft woolly coat gives it

the appearance of being somewhat larger than it actually is. Its ancestry consists of dwarf breeds and Angora. The woolly coat should be up to 7.5 cm (3 in) long. However, it is not suited to commercial spinning due to the high number of guard hairs. These make its fur easier to groom than that of the Angora breeds.

Available in a very extensive range of colour patterns, the Jersey has a very bright future, both as a pet and as an exhibition rabbit. However, you should take account of the extra time that must be devoted to grooming before choosing it.

HOLLAND LOP
Standard: USA
Weight: 1.4-1.8 kg (3-4 lb)
Country of origin: Holland
The smallest of the six dwarf and mini lops, the Holland was first conceived as long as ago as 1949 by Adrien De Cock, whose objective was a Mini French Lop. Only after many years (and failures) did he finally achieve his objective. The main breeds used were the French and English Lops crossed with Netherland Dwarfs.

The breed arrived in the USA during 1976 and proved a great hit. It is now one of America's most loved pets. Its lop ancestry gives it a wonderful temperament. The fur is short and sleek, the legs are short but thick and the pendent ears do not reach the floor. It has the distinctive domed crown of the French Lop. Available in an extensive range of colours and patterns, the breed is likely to continue gaining in popularity for some years, and will no doubt be used in the creation of other dwarfs.

MINI DWARF LOP
Standard: UK
Weight: 1.5-1.6 kg (3.25-3.5 lb)
Country of origin: Britain
This breed is to British dwarfs what the Holland Lop is to the USA. It should, in all respects, be

Mini Dwarf Lop: This is sable and marten in colour.

a miniature of the Dwarf Lop, which is its main lop ancestor. Other dwarfs were used in its development to produce a small size. It is a well-muscled, full-cheeked breed. Acceptable in all colours and patterns, the breed, not surprisingly, is extremely popular both as a pet and as an exhibition rabbit.

AMERICAN FUZZY LOP
Standard: USA
Weight: 1.6-1.8 kg (3.5-4 lb)
Country of origin: USA
The development of the Fuzzy Lop, which was not intentional, provides an extra choice for dwarf enthusiasts. It comes in the form of a longhaired, lop-eared breed that is basically a Holland Lop with a somewhat coarse coat of Angora-type wool. It originated when breeders crossed Angoras with Hollands, with the objective of obtaining an improved coat. But, periodically, individuals with Angora coats appeared in litters. Careful interbreeding of these eventually stabilised the new form, and the breed was given full acceptance in 1988. This delightful package comes in a wide range of colours and patterns to meet any taste.

MINI REX
Standard: UK and USA
Weight: 1.6-2.1 kg (3.5-4.5 lb)
Country of origin: USA
Few people could resist this rabbit because it has just about all the features you could want in a small breed – lovely temperament, elegant proportions and that gorgeous velvet-like coat. Not surprisingly, it is steadily chasing the Netherland for the title of most popular diminutive breed in the world.

The Mini Rex was developed in Texas by Mona Berryhill, who noticed a very small youngster in one of her standard Rex litters. This was mated to a Netherland, and after further breeding, the Mini Rex came into being, gaining full recognition in 1988. Unlike most dwarf breeds, the Mini Rex is a duplicate of its larger parental breed. It exhibits no indication of its Netherland Dwarf heritage, so the term 'mini' is most appropriate. The breed's outstanding feature is, of course, its coat, which must be no more than 1.25 cm (0.5 in; USA – $5/8$ in) in length, and as dense and even as possible. The available colour and pattern choice is more than enough to satisfy any owner.

Dwarf Lop: A thickset and well-muscled breed.

DWARF LOP
Standard: UK
Weight: 2-2.4 kg (4.5-5.25 lb)
Country of origin: Holland
Of the small lops in Britain and the USA, this is probably the oldest, having been developed by the same Dutch breeder who produced the Holland Lop. In its general appearance, it is comparable to the French Lop, and so it is a thickset and well-muscled breed. The basal ridge of the ears should be prominent across the skull. The ears are long and broad, the coat is short, but of good length, and very dense. This very appealing little rabbit is available in most colours and patterns. By today's standards, it is hardly a dwarf, and is heavier than some breeds that are not dwarfs; such has been the progression within the pint-sized breeds.

CASHMERE LOP
Standard: UK
2-2.4 kg (4.5-5.25 lb)
Country of origin: Britain
This is a longhaired Dwarf Lop. The coat is dense with good underfur. The topcoat hairs are longer than those of the underfur and should be silky, never woolly. The hair length is 3.8-5 cm (1.5-2 in). All colours and patterns are

Cashmere Lop: Allow plenty of time for grooming.

acceptable. A very attractive breed, but one which requires ample time devoted to its long coat to prevent it from looking bedraggled. The breed is a relative newcomer but has already gained a strong following.

MINI LOP
Standard: USA
Weight: 2.5-2.9 kg (5.5-6.5 lb)
Country of origin: Germany
Other than being heavier, the Mini Lop is very similar to the Dwarf Lop of the UK, but its ancestry is not quite the same. Although the breed no doubt carries Dwarf Lop genes, its direct ancestor is a breed

called the Kleine Widder. This was exported to the USA in 1972 but not until it was renamed did it start to really gain supporters. Its initial colour range was limited, but, by crossings to the French Lop and Standard Chinchilla, it was expanded to its present extensive range. The Mini makes a fine pet, but has slowly lost ground in popularity, as has its British counterpart, in the face of the increasing number of much smaller breeds.

COLOURS AND PATTERNS
In the UK, there are 63 colours and 22 patterns of these

Agouti Netherland Dwarf: This is the natural wild colour.

recognised in rabbit breeds. In the USA, the choice is comparable. Most of these are available within the dwarf and mini breeds, so the potential combinations from which an owner can choose are almost unlimited. Space does not allow a description of all of these. However, a few terms are worthy of explanation, as they will be seen time and again in adverts and rabbit articles.

AGOUTI
This is the normal wild type

colour. It comprises bands of dark and light pigment along each hair shaft, giving a ticked appearance. When the brown-yellow pigment is replaced by white, it creates the popular *Chinchilla* colour pattern.

ALBINO

A rabbit not able to display any colour pigment – it is a pink- or red-eyed white. If the eye is blue, brown or black, these are not albinos, but *Whites*. The albino is not devoid of colour genes; they cannot express themselves visually. Such a rabbit has inherited an albino gene from each of its parents. In the double dose, the albino mutation suppresses all colour genes from being functional, and their presence is thus masked. Albinism is the complete opposite to full colour, and there are intermediate forms between the two, which form a series – see Himalayan.

Agouti Cashmere Lop: This buck is four years old.

MAGPIE
A colour and white.

BROKEN PATTERN
Any recognised colour in combination with white and placed as required for that breed according to its Standard.

DALMATIAN
White body covered with small coloured blotches and patches.

FOX
Similar to the tan, but the tan is replaced by white, and the chest, flanks and feet are ticked with white guard hairs. In the USA, the Silver Fox pattern is called the Silver Marten.

HARLEQUIN
A colour and orange or fawn.

HIMALAYAN
The nose, tail and feet are coloured, the body is white and the eyes pink. This is one of a series of mutations that progress from full colour to albino in the following manner: Full colour;

Harlequin Lionhead: Orange or fawn mixed with a colour.

Siamese (Sable); Himalayan; Blue-eyed White; Albino.

SELF

A single colour all over the body, as with black, white, blue, and lilac.

SHADED

This is a group term that covers varieties such as the Sable and Marten. The colour is darker on the points (nose, ears, tail, feet) and back, but shades to a lighter colour on the flanks and underbelly.

SIAMESE

This well-known cat pattern is called Seal Point (UK) and Sable Point (USA). It is also used to describe the Sable and Smoke Pearl in the shaded patterns of the rabbit hobby.

TAN

This is a pattern in which the inside of the ears, the eye ring, the chest, belly, neck triangle and underside of jowl and tail are a rich tan. The rest of the body is a self colour – black, blue, chocolate or lilac.

Siamese : This follows the well-known cat pattern.

6 *Breeding*

Pet rabbits are not recommended for breeding – there is no shortage of pet-quality rabbits. Every breeder of quality show stock will have these in greater or lesser numbers. These are the individuals sold in pet shops, or direct from the breeder. There is no gain to the hobby in letting lower-standard rabbits reproduce – it merely lowers the overall standards in the hobby and suppresses values.

If you purchased your dwarf as a typical pet, it is better that it remains as such. You will gain experience in caring for rabbits and can later pursue any breeding aspirations with stock of better quality. Adopting this advice, you can carefully plan your breeding operation and have all the accommodation ready. All too often, pet owners rush into breeding, only to become disenchanted once they encounter the hard realities.

DRAWBACKS

The first reality of breeding is that you will need at least three or four extra cages in which to house the offspring, in the event that they do not sell. The space for these cages and extra food will generally mean having an outbuilding. Even a modest programme will be quite costly, and you must never think in terms of turning a profit from your endeavours. That would be a major error. Few breeders ever break even.

The amount of time needed for cleaning and feeding chores will rise dramatically as your stud grows. Then homes must be found for surplus youngsters. This will mean visits to pet shops and advertising because you will soon have more rabbits than you have friends wanting them.

Babies may die and others may require veterinary attention – more cost and worry. Finally, there will be the usual stream of potential buyers telephoning or visiting you. Many of these will take up a great deal of your time, but will not purchase from you. They may call at the most inappropriate times, such as late at night, and others will do so after buying a rabbit from you that becomes ill. Are you really sure you are prepared to cope with all these realities?

INITIAL STOCK
Assuming you are satisfied with your enthusiasm and have the required capital, then you are strongly recommended to visit one or two rabbit shows. At these, you

It is essential to use animals of the highest quality when planning a breeding programme. This is a top-winning Polish buck.

will see most of the colours and patterns available in your chosen breed, and you may see some you did not know about. You may even decide to change the breed you originally considered breeding.

The show is the best place to make contacts for obtaining your first one or two does. It is better not to start with more than two. This enables you to gain practical experience to add to your enthusiasm and facilities, and to develop your stud accordingly. If you keep things low-key, you are less likely to encounter problems of not enough time, money or sales outlets.

It is always best to purchase does that are registered with your national rabbit association. Offspring from these will have better sales potential to those who may wish to exhibit or breed, assuming your own stock has quality. It is not necessary to purchase the most expensive does, but you do want sound, typical females that have the potential to produce exhibition quality.

Purchase from a successful breeder. Tell them exactly what you hope to achieve, so they can supply accordingly. A buck is not needed at this time. When one is,

it is best to use a high-quality stud who can inject his features into your initial line. From his offspring, you could then retain a male to maintain the stud's influence – and so your line will develop.

It is best to purchase young does, but not weanlings. About four to six months is suggested, as you can better establish their quality. They must then have time to settle into their new home before being expected to breed.

MATING

Never attempt to breed from an immature doe, nor one that is ill or recuperating. The consequence will be a major drain on her immature body and may result in weak offspring. The doe should be about six or more months of age, and should be paired to an experienced stud buck of good quality – preferably one that excels in any features that are weak in the doe. It is most important that the buck has a solid temperament and shows no signs of nervousness.

The doe is always taken to the buck for mating as this greatly reduces the risk of fighting, which is more likely if the doe is in her own territory. Rabbits have a breeding cycle – called the oestrus – of about 13 days in every 16. This means they can be mated at almost at any time. The doe is receptive to mating when her vulva changes from white to purple; it will swell and may discharge liquid.

If a doe is unwilling to be mated on a given day, it is best to remove her and try the next day rather than leave her with the buck, when injuries may result. This process may need to be repeated again until she readily accepts the buck. Remove the doe once a mating has been observed.

A repeat mating one hour later has been shown in a study of commercial rabbits to maximise

This young Cashmere doe is five months old, and this is a good age to assess quality.

litter size while minimising offspring born dead. If the repeat mating is not made for two or more hours, it will have a negative effect on litter size, and so should not be undertaken.

GESTATION
From the day the doe is mated, it will normally be 31 days later that she produces her litter. This can vary from 30 to 33 days. After 33 days, a vet should be consulted, as there may be a problem. It is possible to ascertain by about the 12th day after mating whether the doe is pregnant. This is done by palpation of her abdomen when the tiny pea-sized foetuses can be felt. However, this technique requires experienced hands, and so is best effected by your vet or a breeder.

NESTBOXES
If your doe already has separate sleeping quarters in her housing, then a nestbox is not needed. If the cage is open-plan, one should be provided about three or four days before the litter is expected. It should be a little longer than the doe, and two or three inches wider than she is. It should be of sufficient height and with an entrance hole large enough in diameter for her to enter. It can be made of wood or plastic and can be purchased from pet shops or rabbit supply specialists. The doe will line this with hay and fur from her abdomen and chest.

DIET
In the weeks prior to the birth, it is most important that the doe's rations are steadily increased, because extra nutrients are needed to feed the growing foetuses. If the mother is not in peak condition she may resorb the litter, being instinctively aware that she would be unable to rear it. She may also do this if she is in any way stressed. Maiden does may cannibalise part or all of a litter, but will usually be fine with the second litter.

Whenever a female does attack her own offspring, you should always double-check that her environment, health and diet are satisfactory. If she cannibalises her second litter, it is best not to use her for breeding. This trait can be inherent and passed via the male offspring as well as the females.

THE LITTER
The typical dwarf rabbit will have four or five babies, though the potential range is one to eight.

GROWTH AND DEVELOPMENT

A litter pictured a few hours after birth.

A Mini Lop aged one week.

A Dwarf Lop
at ten days,
with eyes
open.

A three-
week-old
Dwarf Lop.

A Lionhead aged four weeks.

A Dwarf Lop at six weeks of age.

The offspring are born blind, deaf and virtually naked, but hair starts to grow by the fourth day. The eyes and ears will be open by about the ninth day, by which time the youngsters are crawling about. Sometime around the 17- to 21-day mark, the offspring will start to leave the nest and to sample solid foods. There are five digits on each foot, but on the front feet one is much reduced and is called the dewclaw.

Once the litter is two or three days old, you must try to inspect the nest when the doe is outside. Rub your hands in floor covering to mask your scent, then look to see if there are any dead or deformed offspring. The latter must be culled with chloroform or by a sharp blow to the head. This is one of the hardest realities of being a breeder. If you cannot accept this aspect, which is always a possibility with litters, do not think of becoming a breeder.

One of the advantages of having two does mated at the same time is that, in the event that a foster mother is needed, you will have one, but only if her own litter number is small. It is always prudent to find out if any other local breeders have litters due, so foster mothers are available. You can, of course, hand-rear the offspring, but this is a long and very tedious task, not recommended to the novice.

REARING
Once out of the nest, you should handle the babies often so they become well used to humans. You will notice that some are more nervous than others, and you should keep only the ones with excellent temperaments for onward breeding – assuming they have good conformation and colour.

IDENTIFICATION
The country you live in will determine the accepted method of permanent identification for exhibition and registration purposes. In Britain, leg bands are used; in the USA, tattooing of the ear. For more details of these you are referred to your national society.

RECORDS
It is most important that you maintain detailed records of each rabbit and litter. These will be invaluable as time goes by in being the history of your stud. They will be useful when planning matings, and in backtracking to

If you breed top-quality stock, you may wish to have a go at showing your rabbits. This is an orange coloured Dwarf Lop.

find genetic problems, should they suddenly become manifest. Each record card should indicate the individual's registration or other number, its date of birth, its parents, its sex, its colour pattern, its adult weight and the date it died. It may also show when it was mated, but this is usually detailed on breeding cards.

EXHIBITION

A rabbit exhibition is the hobby showcase. It is an opportunity for breeders and owners to compare their stock in a competitive framework. But it is also a very social occasion, and one at which clubs, rabbit product sellers and manufacturers display their wares. Shows range from very small local affairs to the annual national exhibitions, at which the best stock in the country is on view.

The stock of successful exhibitor/breeders is normally much sought-after, but the cost of achieving such status is high, as is the amount of time devoted to building a reputation. But you can exhibit at a low-key level by attending local shows, which will certainly help in building your name in your region, thus increasing sales of your stock.

By attending a number of shows, you can decide whether exhibiting is for you. If so, you will find other exhibitors only too happy to help you.

Joining your local rabbit club is another way to develop knowledge and to gain valuable contacts. If you do not have time to exhibit, but would like your stock to be shown, you could form a partnership with an exhibitor who handles the show side while you attend to the breeding side.

The foregoing text is only intended as a primer on the subject of breeding. The serious hobbyist is recommended to seek more detailed books and information before embarking on a breeding programme, no matter how small this may be. In particular, genetics and practical breeding problems should be given special consideration.

NATIONAL ORGANISATIONS

British Rabbit Council
7 Kirkgate
Newark
Nottinghamshire
NG24 1AD

American Rabbit Breeders
Association, Inc.
PO Box 426
Bloomington
IL 61702

7 *Health Care*

While it is always possible that the most well-cared-for rabbit can become a victim of serious illness, its chances of being so are infinitely less likely than with pets or breeding stock whose owner is lax with their husbandry techniques. This being so, the best way to avoid problems is always to be thinking in terms of preventative strategies. This means that day-to-day chores must be diligently attended to and never allowed to lapse. This is when pathogens get the needed opportunity to proliferate. Breeders are at much greater risk of problems than pet owners are, simply because they are maintaining larger numbers of rabbits in confined spaces. All too often, they expand their stud beyond their ability to cope, either in available time, capital and/or facilities. Once on this path, it is then only a matter of time before a serious illness becomes rampant.

STRATEGY

Management strategy covers three basic areas of husbandry. One consists of the hygiene standards, which encompass all aspects of maintaining the rabbit, conducive to good to health and thus minimising problems. The second is recognising ill health in its earliest stages. The third is how to react once an illness is suspected or diagnosed.

The matter of diagnosing and treating an illness, especially a disease, is the one area of husbandry that the owner is strongly advised not to attempt. Many diseases have clinical signs that are similar to such common things as colds and diarrhoea. If an owner attempts to diagnose and treat, there is the very real danger they may have made an error. Not only have they allowed the pathogen time to increase its numbers, but any treatment given might actually be harmful.

Many problems can only be diagnosed by blood and faecal analysis. Most medicines can only be used for a limited time before they result in negative side effects, such as destroying beneficial gut and other bacteria. By avoiding a vet bill you may be committing your pet to suffering and death – it really is not worth it. Always talk to your vet.

HYGIENE

I am sure you would not wish to live near, let alone in, an open sewer. Yet, relatively speaking, many rabbits have to do almost this within the confines of their housing. It is vital that the pet's home is maintained in a very clean state. It must be totally stripped and cleaned every week – floors, walls and mesh. Floors should be cleaned more often if this is clearly needed.

Food and water vessels should be cleaned daily. Any that become chipped, cracked or very worn should be replaced. Breeders should ensure that feed and water containers are always placed into the same cage they came from – they can easily be numbered. Removed floor debris should never remain in the vicinity of the rabbits; it should be burned or otherwise trashed. Likewise, never allow compost heaps or similar rubbish to be located anywhere near a rabbitry. Bacteria, fungus and flies would be a constant danger.

Personal cleanliness is crucial. Always wash your hands before and after preparing the rabbit's food, after cleaning, gardening, indeed before and after any involvement with your pets. Breeders should wear nylon overalls.

CLINICAL SIGNS

Only by handling your pet every day will you notice the first physical and especially behavioural signs of illness. Always watch your pet when it is feeding, so you know what its favoured items are and whether it is a dainty or a gluttonous eater.

Any abnormal features are clearly an indication of a problem. These include runny eyes or nose, closed eyes, diarrhoea, blood-streaked urine, sores, wounds, lumps, swollen abdomen, and bald patches. Behavioural signs of illness are undue lethargy, excessive sleeping, excessive scratching, sudden increase or decrease in food or water intake, untypical aggression or unwillingness to be

handled – indeed, any behaviour that is not normal for your pet.

REACTION

Once a problem is obvious or suspected, the first thing to do is to isolate the rabbit from all others, and from other pets. These may become infected, or they may be the source of the problem

The condition may only be minor, or the signs may be the first of a serious disease. As a general guide, the more signs displayed, the more serious the problem. Once the patient is isolated in a warm, draught-free location, the next thing is to call the vet and to relate your concerns. The vet will advise you of what to do and whether a visit to the surgery is needed. If so, gather some of the rabbit's faecal pellets and place them in a small plastic container so they are available for microscopy.

If wounds are involved, these should be carefully cleaned and treated with an antiseptic lotion. Whether or not they should be bandaged will of course be determined by their severity. You have now done all you can in this stage of the situation and the next

thing is to effect the vet's treatment based on his or her diagnosis. This should be attended to exactly in line with the vet's instructions, never stopping the treatment just because the pet appears to be getting better.

QUARANTINE

Breeders should ensure that they have a quarantine facility, once their programme is underway, so that any future rabbits added to the stud can be isolated and observed. It should be as far away from the main stockroom as possible. It does not matter how good a home, or stud, additions come from; they must still be subject to quarantine. The period

of this should be 14 to 21 days, which should allow any incubating illness to manifest itself.

During this time, the rabbit's eating and general demeanour can be observed and any small changes to the diet effected. Some breeders routinely worm and treat all newcomers for parasites. The breeder/exhibitor is wise to have two buildings for stock if they are regular exhibitors. The extra cost is an insurance against introducing pathogens from stock returning from a show. Few breeders actually do this, but by not doing so they are taking a major risk that, one day, they might deeply regret. Both pet owners and breeders should always have a first aid kit, while a dull emitter heat lamp and stand is always worth owning.

HEATSTROKE

It is vital that a rabbit is never left in an environment that might induce heatstroke. Examples would be in a vehicle with the windows closed on a hot day, in a hutch left in direct sunshine that results in high internal temperature, or in home cages located where direct sunshine could create excess heat.

Heatstroke in the pet can be recognised by very heavy panting, staring eyes, and finally, total collapse. Should this ever happen, the first thing to do is to move the rabbit to a shaded spot and rapidly bring down its temperature, especially of its head so that brain damage may be avoided.

Soak a cloth in cold water and wipe the head while immersing the body in a bowl or sink. Once the rabbit starts to show signs of revival, it should be gently towelled and then placed in a warm spot to dry. It would be prudent to let the vet inspect it so that it can be treated for shock.

STRESS

Stress may not directly kill a rabbit, but it does lower the efficiency of the immune and other systems. This increases the potential for illness and syndromes. What stresses one rabbit may not do so to another, making it a difficult condition to identify specifically as causal where a disease or malady is concerned. Essentially, however, by appreciating what things cause stress, they can be avoided. Major stress-causing factors are as follows:

- Overcrowding within individual cages.
- Excessive cold and especially excessive heat or continual uncomfortable temperatures.
- Fluctuating temperatures.
- Unclean living conditions.
- Inadequate diet.
- Being housed with a rabbit that is a bully.
- Being housed where cats and dogs can pose a believed (if not real) threat to the pet.
- Inadequate or fluctuating light/dark cycles.
- Noise from machinery.
- Incorrect handling.

In each case the correction is obvious from the problem itself.

SYNDROMES

These are unnatural behaviour patterns that may be induced by stress, or may be the result of other causes. When related to stress, the behaviour pattern is the rabbit's subconscious attempt to compensate, as in pacing in its cage to alleviate boredom and lack of exercise. When syndromes are caused by other factors, such as a dietary deficiency, they can result in self-mutilation, cannibalism of infantile offspring, eating of floor covering and of faecal matter, as well as in increased aggression or shyness, which are usually associated with lack of water.

Syndromes can usually be overcome simply by correction of the underlying problem. But some, such as self-mutilation and fur chewing, may become habit-forming. As such they are more difficult to overcome, even when the diet or other cause is corrected. Clearly, syndromes are best avoided in the first place. This again comes back to the need to ensure that management strategy takes account of all likely problems, their causes, and consequences.

USEFUL DATA

Rectal Temperature: 38.5 to 40 degrees C, with 39.5 degrees C being normal
Heartbeat Rate: 123-304 per minute (Average 205)
Respiratory Rate: 39 per minute
Chromosome #: Diploid 44
Dental Formula: I 4/2 C 0/0 PM 6/4 M 6/6 3D 28 Teeth
Longevity: 6 to 8 years is typical.